What Ted Did

The Story of America's Most Prolific Serial Killer, Ted Bundy

Frances J. Armstrong

Introduction

Picture in your mind a serial killer. Think of someone who has reached the depths of human evil, who has not only committed murder but has done it over and over again. Think of the person who can commit acts of such brutality than even their very name conjure fear, yet whose heinous reign of terror earned them a place in the history books and our collective consciousness. Is this person a man, or a woman? We have multiple documented cases of both.

The body type, it doesn't matter much? Ed Kemper was a huge man, nearly seven feet tall and build like an ox. Dahmer was skinny and shy. But what do you imagine the feeling you'd get off of a serial killer? Would his very presence scream evil? Would you be able to tell, deep in the back of your mind, that the being that stood before you was not another person like you, or like anyone you knew; but that this person was a creature. A creature of evil? What if that person did not have this aura of menace? What if this thing that walked among us was indistinguishable from a normal person? They had no lazy eyes or menacing size, no awkwardness about them. In fact, what if this person were handsome? Instead of some basement dwelling monster living on rats, this was a man that had good skin and find hair, who had a reassuring and calm voice, and a face that seemed friendly. This is not a science fiction story, as this story is not the story of a chameleon or shapeshifter. Such a man once walked among humanity, undetected even as he committed his awful crimes.

His name was Ted Bundy

Birth of a Killer

The child who would become Ted Bundy was born on November 24, 1946, in the bucolic town of Burlington, Vermont. His birth name was Theodore Robert Cowell. He was not born into a happy home, or even a home at all. He was born in the Elizabeth Lund Home for Unwed Mothers, a sort of asylum for the women who had found themselves single and pregnant in a time when being in such a state could lead to them being kicked out of their homes by family. His mother was Eleanor Louise Cowell, known by most simply as Louise. She was twenty two years old when Ted was born. The nature of Ted's paternity, however, has long been a subject of doubt.

On Theodore Cowell's birth certificate, the name Lloyd Marshall was given as the name of his father, a local salesman and veteran of the World War Two air force. But there was never any contact between Ted and Lloyd, and even his mother Louise would in later years change the story of Ted's paternity. On some occasions, she would give the name of Ted's father as Jack Worthington, a sailor that she claimed she was "seduced" by. Lacking a father in any form would damage Ted. FBI studies have shown that 43% of serial killers lacked one of their parents. But there is a darker theory regarding Ted Bundy's paternity that goes beyond lies and absenteeism.

Members of Ted's extended family long held the belief, and the idea has become part of Bundy lore, that Ted was actually fathered by his grandfather in some dark incestuous act on his own daughter. From what we know about Louise's father, that would be not out of his character. There are a few accounts as to how he learned the truth of his birth. He once told a girlfriend that a cousin, in a fit of childish bullying, had called Ted a "bastard" and showed him the birth certificate as proof. His biographers were told that he dug it out himself. One account even states that he didn't learn the truth for years, not until he had reached adulthood. No matter how he learned the truth, Ted carried with him a deep sense of resentment towards his mother for hiding this from him and making no effort to tell the truth.

After his birth, Ted was left in Vermont in the care of relatives while his mother went to her hometown of Philadelphia. For three months they were separated, but eventually Louise retrieved Ted and they moved in with Louise's parents. For three years they lived with Samuel and Eleanor Cowell. There, he was not raised as a grandson. Samuel Cowell adopted baby Ted in the hopes that he could avoid being judged for his birth out of wedlock. Subsequently, Ted was presented to the world as a new Cowell child, a younger brother to Louise. As a young boy this was all Ted knew. Even after learning that his "parents" were actually his grandparents, Ted Bundy showed little negativity towards them when discussing his early life. By his own description, Eleanor Cowell was a timid woman who did what her husband said, a shut in who would get electro-convulsive therapy to treat depression. If accounts of her husband are true, both her obedience and depression are explainable.

By accounts within and without the Cowell family, Samuel Cowell was not a model parent. Samuel was a bigot who hated blacks, the Irish, Italians, and Jews. He was a schizophrenic who spoke to invisible people. He abused the people around him, beating his wife and dog in equal measure. He was easily angered, especially when Ted's paternity was even mentioned. He tossed the neighborhood over his fence by the tail when it had wandered into his yard one too many times. He once threw his younger daughter Julia down a set of stairs simply because she had overslept. Despite all this, Ted looked up to Samuel and even began to identify with him.

The chaos of the Cowell household already was having an effect on young Ted. He developed an early interest in the macabre, particularly death. His aunt, or in his mind at the time his "sister," Julia said that she once awoke with her bed covered in knives. The surrounded her and were inches from her skin. As she lifted her head to look at the foot of her bed, she saw Ted standing there with a huge grin on his small face.

Ted's life changed again in 1950, when his mother changed her last name to Nelson and decided to move west to be with family. It was here, in Tacoma, Washington, that Louise met John Bundy at a church dating night. In 1951, the two were married and John officially adopted young Ted, who for the first time went by the name he was famous for. By now, six year old Ted had developed a new quirk in his personality. He had become obsessed with materialism and wealth. Reportedly the young boy was embarrassed to no end at how little money his new stepfather made in the military. Ted was even ashamed at the idea of someone in his family driving a "sensible" like a Rambler. He even would drag his mother around town, making her look with him into the shop windows of the most expensive stores in Philadelphia.

Ted had a complex relationship with both of his parents. He and John were never close, with Ted himself insisting upon calling his stepfather by his name instead of any sort of familial name. While John made every effort to include Ted on family outings, Ted always complained about feeling left out by a man who he described as "not very bright." Ted also made no effort to befriend any of his four half-siblings. Ted and Louise, on the other hand, were incredibly close. He remained confused about their relationship as a boy, referring to Louise as both his mother and his sister. Despite the lingering resentment Ted held towards his mother, she defended Ted as long as she lived. Even after his confession, trial, and eventual conviction Ted Bundy's mother never stopped defending him as an innocent man. Despite the complexity of Ted's emotions towards his parents, his time after leaving the Cowell household was calm and free of abuse.

Portrait of The Killer As A Young Man

In his youth, Ted was described very positively by his peers. He was described as a bright and happy child, very social and popular with his peers and in good academic standing. But once Ted hit puberty he began to exhibit some truly strange behavior.

While in Tacoma, Ted recalls doing many odd things around town, many of them stemming from a pubescent obsession with women and a growing voyeuristic streak. He would wander through town at night, rummaging through trash barrels and dumpsters in the hopes of finding nude pictures of women. On these searches, he also collected crime novels detective magazines, especially those that described instances of sexual violence. He too particular interest in the publications that contained gory illustrations of the dead or maimed victims. Some nights he would get drunk and wander through his neighborhood, looking for uncovered windows through which he could view women in states of undress.

At school, Ted himself attested that he had no friends and kept largely to himself. While he still was well known in the school, described by classmates as a "medium sized fish in a large pond," he was not as universally popular as he had been when he was younger. His grades suffered. He grew more and more withdrawn as time went on as his nightly sojourns increased, becoming tongue tied in social situations. His nervousness was not limited to meeting women, but to any new people he met. His only sport was skiing, which he practiced using stolen gear. By senior year of high school, Ted had been arrested for burglary and auto theft and had garnered a reputation as a bit of a weirdo. His complex inner self would continue to plague him in college.

In 1965, Ted Bundy started college at the University of Puget Sound before transferring within the year to the University of Washington in Seattle. His major was Chinese. It was here that Ted met his first love, a fellow student named Stephanie Brooks. She was a beautiful young woman who wore her dark hair long and parted down the middle. For a couple years, Ted was content.

But by 1968, Ted had grown dissatisfied with college and dropped out. He began bouncing from minimum wage job to minimum wage job. He also made his first stab at politics, volunteering at Nelson Rockefeller's local office and attending the 1968 Republican National Convention as a delegate for Rockefeller. But by this time, Stephanie had become fed up with Ted's seemingly static career trajectory. She left him in the middle of the year, going home to California and leaving Ted devastated. The one thing that really was going well for the young man had gone bust, and he decided to leave Washington and start drifting across the country. He decided to head east to Philadelphia to see his family, stopping in Arkansas and Colorado.

In Philly, he attended a semester at Temple University and, according to some accounts, may have finally learned the truth about his parentage. But by fall 1969, Ted was back in Washington where he met divorcee Elizabeth Kloepfer (who Bundy has given such names as Meg Anders, Beth Archer, or Liz Kendall) with whom he would maintain a tumultuous on and off relationship for many years. But for the time, Ted seems to have stabilized with the help of Liz and his mother, who supported him even with young children still to take care of.

In 1970, Ted started to turn himself around. He re-enrolled at UW as a psychology major, where he made the honor roll and became a favorite of many of his professors. In 1971, he joined the local suicide crisis hotline, where he befriended an ex-police officer named Anne Rule, who would famously write *The Stranger Beside Me* about Bundy's life and crimes. She says that he was a kind and empathetic man, who was very successful on the line with potential suicides. He was, she says, very understanding of the people he talked to and always seemed interested in them on a personal level.

In 1972, Ted graduated and returned to politics via the reelection campaign of incumbent Governor Daniel J. Evans. He worked as an undercover agent of sorts, following Evans's opponents from place to place and recording their speeches, providing important opposition research for Evans's campaign. After Evans's successful reelection, Ted was hired by the Washington State Republican Party as an assistant to the chairman, Ross Davis. Davis described Bundy as smart and aggressive, as well as someone who "believed in the system." In 1973, Bundy visited California. There he met up with Stephanie Brooks again. Impressed by his newfound ambition and professional bearing, Stephanie restarted her relationship with Ted.

From this point, Ted would maintain his relationship with both Brooks and Kloepfer. Thanks to their geographic distance from each other and Ted's manipulative character, neither woman knew about the other's existence. After being accepted to the University of Puget Sound's School of Law, Ted continued his affair with Brooks. She even flew in on weekends to see him and he regularly introduced her to people, including his boss Ross Davis, as his fiancee. The two of them were discussing marriage but then suddenly something changed.

In January 1974, a few months after Ted and Stephanie rekindled their relationship, he suddenly ceased communication with his almost fiancee. Calls were ignored of dropped. Letters were not returned. It took until mid-February for her to finally reach Ted, finally reaching him over the phone. Stephanie, understandably, was furious with Ted. She demanded that he tell her why he had stopped talking to her, why he'd gone silent. Elizabeth heard the line go quiet. Then, slowly and quietly, Ted responded. He said in a calm, even voice

"Stephanie...I don't know what you're talking about."

He then abruptly hung up, leaving Brooks in stunned silence. They never spoke again. Brooks has stated that, looking back, the whole experience was simply Ted's revenge for breaking up with him in 1968. Ted's given reason?

"I just wanted to prove to myself that I could have married her."

Soon after, Ted started skipping his law classes. He soon dropped out of school for the final time. Then, all over the Pacific Northwest, women one by one started disappearing.

First Blood

When it comes to Bundy's victim list, his early kills are in question. Thanks to Ted's conflicting accounts to multiple biographers and journalists and the less than stringent criminology of the time, we do not have true confirmation of Ted Bundy's pre-1970 crimes. Prior to his execution, he readily confessed to multiple murders but never went into details. The kidnappings and murders he variably confessed to or was accused of, but was not convicted for, include:

- A 1969 kidnapping in Ocean City, New Jersey

- A 1969 pair of murders in Atlantic City New Jersey, committed while visiting family.

- A 1972 murder in Seattle

- A 1973 murder of a hitchhiker near Tumwater, Oregon

- A 1961 kidnapping and murder of a six year old girl, when Bundy was only 14.

Our first confirmed violent act by Ted Bundy was in 1974, when he was twenty seven. Whether he had killed by this point or not, Bundy attested that by this point he had mastered the ability to commit crimes up to and including murder in a way that was able to baffle the primitive forensics of the time.

It is January, 1974 in the dead of the cold Washington winter, a man later identified as Bundy broke into the basement apartment of 18 year old University of Washington dance student Karen Sparks. Quietly opening her window, he methodically unscrewed a metal rod off of her bed frame while she lay unawares. Gazing down at the sleeping woman, Bundy registered no emotion as he raised the rod above his head and brought it down onto her prone body, striking her multiple times on the head. Satisfied that she was sufficiently dazed, Bundy then sexually assaulted her with the same rod. The penetration by the sharp piece of metal caused multiple internal injuries. Bundy made sure to hide his presence before slinking out the way he came. The attack left Sparks with severe and permanent brain damage. She spent ten days in a coma, and the rest of her life with severe disabilities.

Ted's first successful kill took place a month later, in an eerie replication of Bundy's attack on Karen Sparks. Like Sparks, Lynda Anne Healey lived in a basement room and was a student at UW. Bundy was no doubt aware of her beforehand due to her involvement in the local radio station, where she broadcast weather conditions for skiers in the nearby Cascades. Ted followed her for an unknown amount of time before striking. That night, he waited outside for the right moment. He may have been noticed, briefly, by Lynda's roommates who reported seeing a "shadow" outside their window that night. They went to bed thinking it was nothing.

When they woke up the next morning their roommate was gone.

In the night, Bundy had snuck into Lynda's room and bludgeoned her to death. Then, her bed still dripping with blood, he gathered a blouse, blue jeans, and a pair of boots from Lynda's closet. All they found of her in the aftermath was her skull. Between Sparks and Healey, who lived only 11 blocks from each other, the neighborhoods around the university went on virtual lock down. Students, female ones especially, didn't go out at night and locked their doors in fear of what may happen to them. But despite their caution, women would keep disappearing at the hands of Ted Bundy. And he was just getting started.

The disappearances the would follow came with disturbing regularity. Once per month a young woman, all of the same age and look as Bundy's first two victims, would disappear without a trace. In March, 19 year old Donna Gail left her dormitory at Evergreen State College to go to a jazz concert. She never made it to the concert.

On April 17, Susan Elaine Rancourt disappeared on her way to a movie. Like the previous victims, Elaine was a student, in her case Central Washington University. Bundy was steadily working his way south, now 110 miles south of Seattle.

On May 6, Roberta Parks disappeared while on her way to a coffee date at the Student Union. She was a student at Oregon

State University, Corvallis, located 260 miles south of Seattle.

On June 1, 22 year old Brenda Bell disappeared after leaving the Flame Tavern, near the Seattle-Tacoma International Airport. In one of the earliest examples of what would become identified as Bundy's MO, she was last seen speaking to a brown haired man with his arm in a sling.

Bundy's next kill in the Northwest was in his own proverbial backyard, killing a UW student named Georgann Hawkins. Unlike the previous kills , the disappearance of Hawkins occurred in a brightly lit alleyway between her boyfriend's house and her sorority house.

A Developing MO

Just as the death of Lynda Healey and attack on Karen Sparks sent their small neighborhood in Seattle into a panic, Bundy's bloody swath across the northwest became the biggest source of fear for the whole region in that time. Police departments in the cities where the six women had disappeared scrambled to find something, anything that they could use to connect to the as yet unidentified killer. Thanks to Bundy's meticulous execution of his crimes, the investigators had a severe paucity of evidence. In the instance of Georgann Hawkins, three detectives and a forensic scientist combed the alley where she disappeared. They came up empty handed. But even the limited information passed along by the press sent shivers down the spine of the people of Oregon and Washington. Not only were the normal precautions of locked doors and unofficial curfews put in place, but hitchhiking, especially by women (still incredibly common in the early 70's), took a sharp drop.

The few pieces of evidence that the police had were not given to the press, with only the least amount of information given out for fear that being too open would compromise their investigation. But even with their limited evidence, they began to get an idea of Bundy's modus operandi.

Up until this point, all of the disappearances had occurred at night. All of them happened near exam time, when much of the school would be too busy studying to make notice of anything odd happening. All of the victims were young women with dark hair. All of them wore slacks or blue jeans. Most significantly, there was at nearly every crime scene eyewitness accounts that the same man had appeared nearby preceding the disappearance. Starting with Donna Gail in March, a man with brown hair was seen, his arm in a sling, driving a brown Volkswagen Beetle. Sometimes he introduced himself as Ted, often he was asking for help moving some heavy object into his vehicle whether it be books or bags or otherwise.

He would keep a heavy weapon, usually a crowbar, within reach when he and his target got to the car. When he had them where he wanted them, he would beat them and handcuff them into his car. Finally, at the site he did all manner of things to them which would vary by victim. Finally, after they were dead, he'd strip them and deposit their bodies somewhere remote. He'd later donate their clothes to charities, often Goodwill. Ted had become a fully fledged serial killer, and he was just getting started. The police had a dark name for Bundy's victim list: The Girl of the Month Club, so named due to Ted's work rate. From this point until his first arrest in 1977, Ted would kill on average once a month.

By day, Ted was working as a government bureaucrat at the Washington State Department of Emergency Services, where he worked as part of the agency that searched for, ironically, missing and disappeared women. He had broken up with

Elizabeth Kloepfer yet again and was now dating Carol Anne Boone, a double divorcee with children.

Ted's final attack in the Pacific Northwest happened on Sunday, July 14th. His boldness had grown, as this attack occurred in broad daylight. His hunting ground was the Lake Sammamish State Park, about 20 miles east of Seattle. Ted stuck to his usual act. Introducing himself as Ted, his arm in a sling and with a slight affected accent, he asked women on the beach if they would give him a hand with a sailboat he had needed to unload from his Volkswagen Beetle. Even with the limited information that the press had, the female population was on edge. Four women he asked turned him down flat. The fifth agreed to go with him. They got as far as the parking lot. When she spotted the Volkswagen and didn't see a sailboat anywhere in sight, she bolted.

He then approached Janice Ott, a newlywed juvenile case worker who had moved to Seattle for work, leaving her husband behind in California. She had studied anti-social personality disorders in college, and, ironically, she wanted to help people just like Ted to overcome their mental illness before it was too late. But it turned out to be too late to her. The 23 year old blonde, lonely and missing her husband, fell for the handsome man begging for help. Once they got to Ted's Beetle, he was able to restrain her and stuff her into his car. He didn't kill her, though. He had something else planned.

Ted returned to the beach, his trap sprung but his blood lust not sated. He lurked around the park, waiting for the right victim. When Denise Naslund got up from a picnic with her boyfriend to go to the bathroom, Ted found his victim. A 5 ft 4 in brunette studying to be a computer programmer, Denise walked off with her dog. The dog came back alone. Forcing Denise back to his car, or perhaps knocking her out and dragging her there, Ted drove off to his killing place. Once there, he made Ott watched as he butchered Naslund in front of her before moving on to kill her as well.

This incident at the lake was finally enough for the King County police to go public with details of Bundy's MO and a composite sketch. Many of the people that Bundy had met in his life in Seattle recognized the face of the man in all the papers. Anne Rule, Ted's ex Elizabeth, and Ted' s coworkers all called in to point the finger at hiim But thanks to the sensational nature of the crime and the sheer scale of them, the police were inundated with up to 200 tips a day. Bundy, a handsome young law student with no criminal record, didn't tick any of the boxes in a spree killer profile.

In September, two hunters found a pair of skeletons on a service road two miles away from Sammamish, along with an extra femur and several vertebrae. Six months later, some university students found the skulls of four of his victims in the forest east of Issaquah. But by the time all of this was being discovered, Ted was long gone. He would now move east, leaving blood and gore in his wake.

Bundy In The Mountains

Ted Bundy was a driven man, convinced of his own intelligence with his eye towards success. So, in 1974, he decided to take another chance attending law school. When he applied previously, he'd gotten into the University of Puget Sound and the University of Utah. He'd decided at that time to go to UPS, where he could stay involved in local politics and juggle the women he was dating.

But on his second go, Ted didn't want to stay close. He already had some heat with the police after the publication of the police sketch, and he didn't want to risk staying close to his murders any longer. So when he received his second acceptance to the University of Utah Law School, he jumped at the chance. In August, he packed up his belongings and moved to Salt Lake City. Elizabeth Kloepfer, his on again off again girlfriend, recently back together with Ted, was left behind in Seattle. They continued to talk on the phone, but Ted had no real devotion to Elizabeth. By his account, the charismatic and handsome Bundy dated dozens of women while still ostensibly dating Elizabeth long distance.

But despite the chance he had received in attending law school a second time, Ted ran into a roadblock quite quickly. The curriculum he had to take for his first year of law was nearly incomprehensible to Ted. The classes were too hard, he said, and his classmates he felt had advantages over him academically and intellectually. When describing his feelings on this turn of events,

Ted called it a disappointment. Perhaps and understatement, considering what his frustration at the turn of events would lead to.

Ted couldn't just run away from his violent urges, and it was not long before his frustrations with law school bubbled up into violence yet again.

His first kill took place in Idaho, preying yet again on a hitchhiker. Nothing is known about this victim beyond the fact Bundy raped and strangled her before leaving her in the wilderness. He came back the next day with a camera, taking pictures as he slowly dismembered the body and dumping the remains in a nearby river. They were never recovered.

His first named kill at this stage in his life was Nancy Wilcox, on October 2nd. Unlike his previous kills up until now, or at least the ones we have confirmation of, Nancy was not in college or even college age. Though she fit his "type" of young brunettes, she was only 16 and still in high school at the time of her death. She was kidnapped by Bundy in her home suburb of Holladay, and she was last seen in a bug very similar to the one that had been identified as Bundy's before her disappearance. He drove her into a secluded bit of forest where he intended to rape her and let her go. This act, according to Bundy, was an attempt to suppress his pathological urges. But it didn't end there.

Understandably terrified, Nancy's screams echoed throughout the forest and Bundy acted quickly to quiet her. He wrapped his hands around her throat and squeezed. By Bundy's recollection, he was not trying to kill the girl. But intentionally or no, Bundy's grip was too tight and held too long and Nancy Wilcox quickly was strangled to death. He buried her remains a in patch of forest 200 miles south of the place from where he had taken her, an area near the remote Capitol Reef National Park. Despite Bundy's identification of her burial spot, investigators never found any piece of Nancy Wilcox.

He next set his sights on Melissa Smith, the 17 year old daughter of the Chief of Police for Midvale, Utah. Like Holladay, Midvale was a small town of tightly knit Mormons that acted as a suburb for Salt Lake City. In a safe town like this with her father as chief, the 5'3 Melissa probably felt no fear walking around her small town at any hour. But on the night of October 18th, 1975, that changed. That night she had plans to stay at a friend's house overnight. She stopped off a pizza parlor to console a friend who'd had a fight with their boyfriend before leaving to get her overnight clothes and toiletries from her house. She never made it there. Her body was found nine days later, naked and bearing the marks of rape, sodomy, and strangulation. The gashes and bruises covering her body came from repeated beatings with a crowbar. An autopsy revealed that the 17 year old had been kept alive for 7 days before her death. Before his execution, Bundy detailed the strange ritual he undertook with Smith's corpse. Once she was dead, he began to give her what could only be considered a makeover. He shampood, brushed, and styled her hair, still tangled from struggle and matted by blood. Her body was found in the Wasatch Mountain, ten days after her disappearance.

A similar murder occurred not even two weeks later. 17 year old Laura Aime was brunette like Melissa, but tall and very thin. An insecure high school dropout, she was a drifter who worked odd jobs around Lehi, Utah before Bundy took her. She'd gone to a cafe on Halloween night, but left at midnight and went to the park. There was no accident in the killing of Aime. He deliberately tortured, raped, and beat her, again with a crowbar, before very quickly and quietly dispatching her with a pair of nylon stockings. Like the corpse of Melissa Smith, Aime's corpse had been violated repeatedly post mortem was well as done up with makeup and shampoo. Her body was found on Thanksgiving Day, in a nondescript canyon nine miles north of Lehi.

Eight days later, Ted Bundy made his first major slip up. The would-be victim was an 18 year old telephone operator named Carol Daronch. She met Bundy ithe mall. She had been there to visit with cousins, and had left them to buy a book at the local Walden's Books. There, a handsome man in a police uniform approached her between the shelves. This was a new tactic for Bundy, who until now has banked on his good looks and natural charisma to lure in his victims. But in some cases his normal ruse of an injured man needing help wouldn't suffice. So he used his love of authority to pretend to *be* an authority, usually a policeman or firefighter. It was in this guise that he lured

Carol Daronch back to his vehicle, a light brown Volkswagen as per Ted's usual taste. He told her that someone had broken into her car and that she needed to come with him to verify the vehicle and do some paperwork. Though she had some misgivings, Bundy was able to ward off any of her defenses. Upon reaching her car, with no damage and nothing missing, Daronch again had questions. Still keeping his act up, Ted then told her that she needed to come "to the station" to ID a suspect. She followed him hesitantly until they came to the back of a building. He called it a station but it was really a laundromat. With no suspect, or police for that matter, in sight, Bundy had to spin his wheels to keep Daronch from questioning further. He had his mark in his clutches, but his cover was quickly unraveling. He decided to move the story along by citing an imaginary "headquarters" as the place where the suspect was. This was how he got her into the Volkswagen. When she got in, she got close enough to the "policeman" to smell alcohol on his breath. Already questioning things, the idea of a policeman driving a Bug finally kicked Daronch's survival instincts into high gear. However, by the time she was ready to escape Ted was already tearing off at a high speed. He told her to put on her seat belt, and she suddenly realized that they were driving, not towards the police headquarters, but *away* from it.

His cover now fully blown, Ted hit his brakes and the small car screeched to a halt. Taking advantage of Daronch's dazed state from the sudden stop, Ted lunged over and tried to handcuff her. Acting partially out of reflex, Daronch snapped out of her daze and quickly struggled with her captor. In such a small car, Daronch put up enough of a fight to throw Ted off. He made the crucial mistake by putting both cuffs on the same wrist. Her hand free and his bounds now occupied, Ted had to appeal to baldfaced violence. Drawing a small pistol from his coat, he threatened to kill her if she didn't go quietly. Undeterred, Daronch fell out of the car. As she lay in the mud, a light rain falling on her face, she saw the dark figure of Ted Bundy emerge from the car. He had a crowbar in his hand.

She tried to scramble away from him, but the thick mud made it hard to move. He picked the small girl up and slammed her into the side of the car. In a sudden burst of adrenaline brought on by her survival instinct, she broke free yet again. She began to run to the road at an uninhibited pace, ignoring the mud and rain and any debris underfoot. She emerged onto the road with Ted right on her tail. Her adrenaline spent, Daronch stood on the side of the road and prayed someone would come. Luckily, someone did. An older couple turned the corner and saw a small woman covered in mud screaming by the side of the road. Taking her terror at face value, the couple let Daronch into their car. They sped off, putting Bundy behind them as quickly as possible. Carol Daronch became the first survivor of Ted Bundy who could attest to his face and his strategy. She would become a valuable source for the now multi-state manhunt.

Bundy slunk away, riled up and now frustrated. Not only had his bloodlust not been sated, but he'd been bested. Bundy was not a man who liked being outsmarted or beaten. So he drove north, stewing in a violent rage as he searched for another victim. He found his release Viermont High School, 19 miles north of the his failure with Carol Daronch. The victim was 17 year old Debby Kent, who was attending a play with her parents. Her brother was at the local ice rink, and it was Debby's job to pick him up when the play finished. Leaving her parents inside to wait, she left. She didn't return, and her brother never saw her at the ice rink. Other students and the drama teacher report a stranger asking them to come identify a broken-in car. One student reported seeing the same man out behind the school, pacing impatiently. But the people within the school thought nothing of these sightings. Even when they heard screams, two long and high screams of someone they described as being full of "mortal terror." A few people even went out and stared into the growing dark, but they saw nothing. As the crowd at the school shrank and the clock inched closer to midnight, Debby's parents and brother became increasingly impatient. When it was midnight proper, the irritated parents emerged from the theater to wait by the curb. But when they saw the parking lot empty save one car, their car, they knew something was up. They called the police. Law enforcement officials were already on edge after the various disappearances and deaths in the surrounding towns. They were quick to set up a crime scene and look for clues. All they found was a key to the pair of handcuffs that Carol Daronch was wearing when she showed up at the Murray, Utah police station. Debby Kent herself was never found, and Bundy never betrayed her final resting place.

Elizabeth Kloepfer, Ted's ex-girlfriend he'd abandoned in his move, was keeping up with his activity. She read the news of the disappearances, still recognizing Ted's MO from his time in Washington. She called the King County police again. Having had time to investigate since they'd dismissed Bundy as a suspect, the police had moved him further and further up the ranks of their suspect list. Unfortunately, their best witness from Bundy's killings at Lake Sammamish did not identify Bundy as the killer out of a photo lineup. In December, she called the

Salt Lake County Sherriff's office and relayed her information to them. They too did not have enough evidence to connect Bundy with the recent string of disappearances. For the time being, Bundy was safe. In early 1975, after his final exams, he returned to Seattle to spend a week with Kloepfer. Not once did she mention her contact with the police, and they made plans for her to come out to Utah later that year.

Ted knew the heat was back on, especially with Daronch's escape. So while he stayed in Salt Lake City to continue his law studies, he moved his murders into Utah's neighbor to the East, Colorado.

Ted's first kill in Colorado happened almost immediately after he left Seattle. His victim was 23 year old nurse named Caryn

Campbell, engaged and planning her wedding. When Ted took her, she was on a ski trip with her fiancee and his two children from his previous marriage. After a long day of skiing in the mountains, they sat in the lounge of the ski lodge to relax after dinner. Caryn, who was nursing a flu at the time, had left a magazine in their room. She didn't return. Noticing her absence, her fiancee went to look for her. Despite his frantic combing of the lodge and room, she was nowhere to be seen. He wouldn't see her again until her corpse appeared a month later by the side of a dirt road just outside of the ski resort. She had been raped repeatedly before being killed with a blunt instrument that left grooves on her skull where it struck. She also had been cut repeatedly by a sharp weapon.

In March of 1975, Bundy struck again in Vail, Colorado, a town 100 miles northeast of where he'd killed Caryn Campbell. Julie Cunningham was a 26 year old ski instructor who also worked at a sporting goods store. He took her while she was on her way to a dinner date with a friend. He approached her on crutches, asking for help getting his ski boots into his car. When they got to the car, he clubbed her over the head and handcuffed her. Then she drove her 90 miles west to Rifle, Colorado, where he raped her and strangled her like he had the others. Unlike the past victims, Bundy didn't leave her to simply rot where he left her. He would return to revisit the remains of Cunningham several weeks later, a six hour drive from Salt Lake City. Again, despite Bundy's confession and identification of her burial site, the body of Julie Cunningham was never recovered.

Denise Oliverson disappeared a month later, on April 6th, in Grand Junction, Colorado, near the Colorado-Utah border. The 25 year old had been on her way to her parents's house after a fight with her boyfriend. All they ever found of her were here bike and sandals under a viaduct near the railroad.

Barring the unconfirmed murder of an 8 year old when he was 15, Bundy's youngest murder occurred on May 6th of 1975. Lynette Dawn Culver was 12 years old and still attending junior high when Bundy took her. This killing occurred in Pocatello, Idaho. Ted had driven 160 miles north to make his next kill, perhaps in an attempt to throw of f the scent. This is further supported by his change in MO. Besides the age difference with Bundy's past victims, he made no attempt to trick her, perhaps being able to simply overpower her. He also didn't take her somewhere remote, instead taking her to a Holiday Inn. He drowned the child in the bath before raping her corpse repeatedly, then dumping her in a nearby river. Her remains were never discovered, and she is officially missing like so many of Bundy's victims. In his confession to her murder, however, Bundy relayed information about Lynette's life and personality that he would only know by talking to her.

In mid-May, shortly after the death of Lynette Culver, three of Bundy's former co-workers at the Washington State DES came to visit. One of them was his former paramour Carol Anne Boone. The trio stayed a week in Bundy's Salt Lake City apartment. A month later, in early June, Bundy again returned to Seattle to stay with Kloepfer. There was no mention of Kloepfer's contact with police, nor did Bundy mention his relationships with Boone and a fellow law student back at the University of Utah.

Shortly after this visit, he would commit his final murder in the West, that of Susan Curtis. Though details are scarce, her murder was his final confession, confessed to right before he entered the execution chamber. Of the disappearances that are attributed to Bundy's murder spree in Utah, six bodies were never recovered.

After his final kill, it seems Ted tried yet again to normalize his life, at least by a little. In early fall of 1975, Ted was baptized into the dominant religious authority in his adopted home state: The Church of Jesus Christ of Latter Day Saints. Ted Bundy had an interesting relationship with religion. Though he made the effort to join the Mormon church, he quickly lapsed. He was a rare sight at services and didn't follow the tenets of the church, especially the tenet abhorring alcohol, which Bundy needed to commit his crimes. But he was, as far as we know, peacefully studying law now. It was a pause in his spree. But it was this pause that gave law enforcement the time they needed to finally catch him.

Ever since Ted left Seattle, the King County police had been struggling to put the pieces of his murders together. Although Bundy had always been fastidious in his attempts to hide his crime, there was still plenty of data for the police to work with. So much, in fact, that it was actually hindering the investigation. There was so much information that it became disorganized and was almost useless.

So the police decided to use a brand new technique to aid their investigation. They assembled one of the first crime databases, all for one man. The technology was so new that they had to use a payroll computer to do it. At that time, computers were huge and incredibly primitive. They input all the information they had- classmates and acquaintances of each person Bundy had killed, known sex offenders, all Volkswagen owners named Ted, etc.- and programmed the computer to search for any coincidences. There were thousands of names that came up in each category, but after the computer's analysis they got twenty six names. One of them was Bundy. They then made a list of one hundred suspects, gleaned from the thousands of often sensational tips, who they thought were their best. Bundy was on that list as well. They worked there way down the list, hoping that they'd finally get their man. But, with Bundy at the literal top of their list, the Utah police got their man.

The Noose Tightens

Like so many successful criminals of the past, it was not his major crimes that did Bundy in. Like Al Capone was finally jailed for tax evasion, Bundy's fatal slip up was failing to pull over for a routine traffic stop. When the police officer walked up to the driver side window, the window came down and he was greeted by a handsome and polite man. Bundy had always trusted the system, even as he worked avoided it, and had no reason to antagonize the police. But the officer noticed something odd about Ted's car. There wasn't a passenger seat. The Highway Patrol Officer wanted to check the rest of the car, and Bundy gave him permission. The officer found several suspicious objects in the trunk and backseat of the small car. He found a ski mask, a mask made out of pantyhose, a crowbar, an ice pick, handcuffs, a coil of rope, several trash bags, and a collection of objects that he assumed to be burglar's tool. Thinking on his feet, the charismatic Ted had a reason for all of these objects. The mask was for skiing, the handcuffs the officer had found were found in a dumpster, and that the rest were just items that he used around the house.

The patrol officer was not convinced by Ted, and insisted on bringing the man in. Once at the station, the information given by the officer and Bundy quickly set off alarm bells. A detective named Jerry Thompson remembered that a car like Ted's and a man matching Ted's description were seen at Viewmont High School the night of Debbie Kent's disappearance.

Combined with Elizabeth Kloepfer's tip earlier in the year, the police had probably cause to get a search warrant for Bundy's apartment. There, they found a preponderance of evidence. Brochures for ski resort with a check next to the resort where Caryn Campbell was staying when she died, a flyer for the same play that Debbie Kent was attending the night of her death. Unfortunately, neither of these were enough evidence to incriminate Bundy. Bundy was released on bail. Bundy says that he had a collection of Polaroids, each depicting his victims at varying stages of their murder, in his utility room. The investigating officers missed these photos, and Bundy swiftly disposed of them when he got back home. But he wasn't truly free yet.

The Salt Lake City police placed Bundy under round the clock surveillance, keeping officers nearby and watching Bundy and his apartment at all times. While Bundy was observed, Detective Thompson and two other detectives caught a flight to Seattle to speak with one of their key informants, Elizabeth Kloepfer. She told them about her life with Bundy. Of particular interest to the detectives was a list of items that Kloepfer said she had discovered and for which Ted had no reason to own. A pair of crutches, surgical gloves, and a bag of plaster of Paris, both of which Ted admitted were stolen from a medical supply company. A meat cleaver which he never used, for cooking at least, that he packed on his move to Utah. She found what she called an "Oriental" knife in one of his coats, and once discovered a bag of women's clothing, clothing that was not hers. The detectives discovered that Bundy was almost constantly in debt, and were told by Kloepfer that everything of value that he owned had been stolen. She'd once confronted him on this, over a suspiciously nice stereo and television. His response was to threaten to snap her neck. He often would wake up in the middle of the night and take a flashlight under their bed covers to examine her body. To Bundy, Elizabeth was something for him to own,something that fed his desire to covet. Elizabeth fit his type, the one established so many years ago by Stephanie Brooks, and any attempt to deviate from this type was met with violence. Elizabeth recounted to the detectives how upset Bundy would get when she wanted to cut her hair, which she kept long and parted in the middle like so many of Bundy's victims. Elizabeth even was an unwitting accessory to Bundy's crimes, as he kept a huge and heavy lug wrench in the trunk of her Volkswagen Beetle, which he borrowed often. The wrench, taped up halfway to prevent the leaving of fingerprints, was put in her car "for protection," according to Ted. Luckily, the detectives were able to confirm that Elizabeth was not an accomplice, as she was not with Bundy on any of the nights of his kills. Satisfied with her responses, the Utah detectives thanked her and returned home. Kloepfer would later speak with a Seattle homicide detective, who filled Elizabeth in on what many consider to be the defining break in Ted Bundy's life, his failed engagement with Stephane Brooks. Until now she never knew of Ted's infidelity, nor did she know that when she and Bundy started their relationship *she* was the other woman.

In September, still under watch by the police, Bundy sold his Volkswagen Beetle to a teenager in the town of Midvale. This was yet another misstep at the hands of Bundy. The police quickly took the car in as evidence, and a thorough search of the car turned up several hairs that did not belong to Bundy. The hairs they found were identical to hair samples taken from Caryn Campbell's body. Though DNA evidence has not become a part of forensic science, they were able to identify hairs from Carol DaRonch and Melissa Smith thanks to matches between microscopic traits of the hairs.

In October, a month after the police positively identified the presence of her hairs in Bundy's car, Carol DaRonch was brought in to look at a lineup containing Bundy. She immediately identified Bundy in the lineup as the man who tried to kidnap her. They subsequently arrested him on charges of aggravated kidnapping and attempted criminal assault. He was released on a $15,000 bail that was paid by his parents and he returned to Seattle to stay with Kloepfer, who took him in despite the new knowledge brought to her attention by the police. The Seattle police were no doubt salivating at the prospect of bringing their man in now that he was back in their jurisdiction. But they lacked the necessary evidence to indict, so they contented themselves with merely watching the man and his girlfriend constantly.]

In November, the various law enforcement agencies searching for Ted Bundy finally joined forces in their investigation. The three detectives spearheading each department's efforts-Jerry Thompson of the Salt Lake City Police, Robert Keppel of the King County Police, and Michael Fisher of Colorado-called a meeting to share information with each other in Aspen, Colorado. This meeting between the three men, together with over thirty detectives and prosecutors from the five states Bundy had operated in, became famous as "The Aspen Summit." The agreement across the board was that Ted Bundy was the man they were looking for, but they lacked the hard evidence they needed to charge him for his heinous crimes.

Ted Bundy finally went before a judge in February of 1976. There was no jury, a right waived by Bundy for fear that the sensational and highly public nature of his case might bias a jury drawn from the public. The trial took four days. After a weekend's deliberation, Judge Stewart Hanson Jr. sentenced Bundy on March 1st, 1976. Bundy was to spend between one and fifteen years at the Utah State Prison. Safely put away, Bundy was seemingly contained. But even as a boxed crook, Ted Bundy was as wily as ever. In October of 1976, Bundy was discovered in the bushes of the prison carrying an "escape kit," consisting of road maps, airline schedules, and a social security card. The prison didn't know how he got hold of these items, but he spent the following weeks in solitary confinement. Lucky for Ted, he'd be out of the Utah prison soon. But it was not on his terms. He would soon be officially charged with murder for the first time, for the killing of Caryn Campbell. Waiving any sort of process for extradition, Ted Bundy was sent to Aspen, Colorado for his trial in that state.

A Non Model Prisoner.

Ted's trial took place in Aspen, at the Pitkin County courthouse. There's a common joke in legal circles that anybody who represents themselves in court is a moron, but Ted's request to be his own attorney for his murder trial came out of base cunning. Thanks to his role as his own lawyer, the judge did not require Ted to be bound during the trial. Free of his handcuffs and ankle cuffs, Ted was unrestrained for the first time in a long time. He wasn't going to waste it.

During the first recess of the trial, Bundy requested access to the courthouse law library ostensibly to do research to help his case. Granted permission by the judge, Bundy was left unsupervised in the library on the second floor of the courthouse. Bundy could now set his plan in motion. Opening a window, he jumped down two stories and onto the courthouse grounds. He did not land well and sprained his right ankle as he did. Shedding his topmost layer of identifiable clothing, Bundy began to make his escape. Limited by his new limp, Ted could only walk through the city of Aspen, easily avoiding the roadblocks that police were quickly setting up in anticipation of a motorized escape. Once he reached the outskirts of Aspen, he turned southward and began to hike up Aspen Mountain. He climbed nearly to the 10, 507 ft peak of the mountain before breaking into a nearby hunting lodge as night fell. He stole some clothes and took shelter in the small wooden cabin, eating some of the food the owner had left behind. The next morning, he packed up some more food and stolen clothes away and grabbed a rifle from the cabin as well. He began again his march south, hoping to reach the town of Crested Butte. Sadly, he over estimated his ability to survive and was quickly lost in the thick Colorado forest. He wandered aimlessly for two days, so lost and frantic that he even missed two separate trails that would have put him back on track to escape. On June 10th of 1977, Bundy came upon a camping trailer. Like the ski lodge, Bundy broke in and took more food and a parka to continue on his journey. It was here, though, that he changed his path. Instead of heading south, he instead turned around and began to walk back north towards Aspen. He stole a car from the Aspen Golf Course and began to head into town, but he was not quite as stealthy as he may have liked. Sleep deprived, frozen from the cold of the mountains, and with a now swollen and near useless ankle shooting pain up his leg every time he tried to move, Bundy's driving was erratic and haphazard. He was an easy target for a pair police, who spotted him weaving in and out of the lane he was driving in. After six days on the lamb, Ted was back in police custody. What may have seemed spontaneous to police was in fact a planned escape. This was proven by the presence of a map in the car, a piece of evidence used by the prosecution to show the location of Caryn Campbell's body. Ted had been using it to find his way around Aspen.

Back in jail, Ted was still itching for freedom. Despite advice from friends and family and a rapidly deteriorating case against him, Ted made plans to escape yet again. Over the next six months Bundy put together the necessary tools for his plan. The easiest tools to get were a hacksaw and floor plan of the jail, gotten from other prisoners. He also collected $500 cash, smuggled in bit by bit by his multiple visitors. His plan to escape was relatively simple. In the roof of his cell were bars that reinforced the ceiling. Using his ill-gotten hacksaw, Ted slowly weakened these bars every night while the rest of the jail was showering. He also watched his food intake closely, dropping 35 pounds so that he could easily fit through the hole he was making and wriggle through the small crawlspace above his cell. He spent several weeks doing practice runs, feeling out his escape route in the darkness unbeknownst to the guards. A prisoner in the cell next to Bundy's tried to tell the guards that there was odd movement in the ceiling, but the guards blew him off. On December 30th, Ted made his move.

It was New Year's Eve, when the jail was half empty and lightly guarded thanks to the holiday. Taking advantage of the skeletal population, Bundy piled books and papers on his bed and then covered them with his blanket in a crude but effective facsimile of his sleeping form. He uncovered the one square foot hole in his ceiling, stood on a chair, and wriggled into the space. He crawled through the space, which connected most of the jail, until he was directly over the apartment of the Chief Jailer who was off celebrating at a New Year's party with his wife. He rummaged through the jailer's closet, stealing a set of street clothes that he quickly changed into them. He walked right out of the jail's front door. By the time the jail noticed his absence, he was already in Chicago.

Bundy Goes Floridian

In some ways, Florida was the perfect place for Bundy to run. Not only was it geographically on the complete opposite end of the country from the place from which he had come, but its extensive swampland and forests meant that bodies were easy to hide and decay quickly. He made his way south first by train, stopping in at Ann Arbor, Michigan to catch the 1978 Rose Bowl, where the University of Washington beat Michigan. Then he stole a car and drove to Atlanta, where he caught a bus to Tallahassee. Under the name Chris Hagen he rented a room near the campus of Florida State University. By Bundy's account, he was trying to start clean and stay on the straight and narrow. But he only ever applied to one job, and he abandoned it once the employer asked for ID. Soon he was back to petty crime to support himself, shoplifting and stealing credit cards. Soon, he would return to his life of violence and the fear of Bundy would soon affect the East coast as it had the West.

It was early morning on January 15th, 1978 when Bundy arrived at the Chi Omega sorority house on the campus of Florida State University. He was barely a week into his Tallahassee residence. He searched the perimeter of the house, using the darkness that still covered the grounds as a cover for his stalking. Bundy was lucky to find a rear door with a broken lock. He was in the silent house, filled with sleeping young women ripe for his picking. The wake up call the sorority sisters received that morning was a nasty one.

He spent some time trying to find the right girl to start with, deciding on Margaret Bowman,21, as his first victim. She had spent the night before on a blind date and eagerly shared the details of said date with her sisters before going to bed. At 2:45 AM, Bundy struck. Taking a piece of firewood from a nearby hearth, he viciously bludgeoned Bowman over the head with it, caving in her skull. He then used some of Margaret's own pantyhose as a makeshift garotte, brought it across her neck, and pulled-strangling her to death. Her strangulation at the hands of Bundy was so violent that her neck nearly broke in his hands. His attack was so swift that none of Bowman's sisters were aware of her death. Ted then moved on, not satisfied with one kill.

His next target was 20 year old Lisa Levy, a sophomore who had spent the evening at a local disco. He used the same piece of firewood, still covered in the blood and brains of Margaret Bowman, to bludgeon Levy unconscious. He strangled her as well, maintaining a small amount of control this time and not as severely maiming her in the process. But he was not satisfied with simply killing her. He tore off one of her nipples and took a large bite out of her left buttock, and shoved a bottle of hairspray into her vagina. He then moved next door to the room of Karen Chandler, 21.

By now, many of the sorority sisters who had been out partying were slowly trickling back home. Attuned to the way their house was supposed to be, they could immediately sense an intruder in their midst.

One sister reported having seen Bundy run past her window, another heard thumping noises above her room. They decided that the prudent thing to do would be to alert their house mother, who lived at the end of the hallway that Karen Chandler lived on. As they rushed down the hallway, they were met by the grisly sight of Karen Chandler stumbling out of her room. She was babbling, half coherent, with blood streaming down her face. Her jaw was broken in several places, she was missing half of her teeth, and one of her fingers was broken. Unbeknownst to the shocked sisters in the hallway, Bundy had also attacked Chandler's roommate, the twenty year old Kathy Kleiner. The housemother, roused by the screams of her charges, rushed out of her room to see the grisly sight of Chandler surrounded by her sisters, pallid with fear. She charged into Chandler's room, where she saw Kleiner sitting calmly on her bed. She had her head in her hands, blood streaming between her fingers. Bundy had broken her jaw in three places, deeply lacerated her face, neck, and shoulder, and given her severe whiplash in a failed attempt at strangulation. Neither she nor Chandler remembered who had done this to them, too tired or in shock to identify Bundy. He slipped out the way he came, unnoticed amidst the chaos.

Even after all of the violence he'd already committed, Bundy wasn't sated. He continued to prowl through the early daylight for another victim. He found one in a basement apartment eight blocks from the Chi Omega house, the apartment of FSU dance student Cheryl Thomas. After staying late with her date from the previous evening, she did not get home until around 1:30 in the morning. She was still sleeping when Bundy entered her apartment. Her neighbor, Debbie, woke to the sound of strange hammering sound coming from below. The whole house seemed to shake at each deafening thump. When they called Cheryl, there was no response from her. After five attempts, Debbie and her roommate decided to call the police. Unaware of the incident at Chi Omega, the two were taken aback at how quickly the police arrived: over a dozen police cars were in front of their house in 4 minutes. The police entered Cheryl Thomas's room to see the tall girl stretched across her bed diagonally, lying in her own blood. She was barely conscious and whispering to herself, her face turning purple and she had suffered multiple serious head wounds. In the attack, Bundy had fractured her skull in five places. She lost hearing in her left ear. Bundy dislocated her shoulder and broker her jaw. The most devastating injury was the severe damage dealt to Thomas's 8th cranial nerve, which meant Thomas never again would have perfect balance. Though lucky to be alive, the scarred Thomas would never dance again. The police found a semen stain on her bed, and a pantyhose mask containing Ted Bundy's hairs.

Bundy waited until February 8th to strike again, driving 150 miles east to Jacksonville in a van he'd stolen from Florida State, still plated and marked as a university vehicle. He approached 14 year old Leslie Parmenter in a parking lot, falling back on his well worn facade as an authority figure. Parmenter was the daughter of the Jacksonville Chief of Detectives, and didn't trust "Richard Burton, Fire Department" one bit. But Bundy persisted until Parmenter's older brother emerged from the business and challenged his credentials. This sent Bundy packing. Frustrated, Bundy spent the afternoon backtracking 60 miles wast to Lake City, a small town notable only for its location at the start of the I-75. It was here that Bundy would make his final kill.

Ted's target was Lake City Junior High, where he parked his car the next morning. He sat and waited for a mark to appear, and finally one did. He spotted her running between two buildings, a small brown hair girl, 5 foot tall and just barely 100 pounds. 12 year old Kimberly Leach had just gotten to her physical education class when her homeroom teacher had called her back. She had left her purse behind. With the permission of her PE teacher, she left to retrieve the purse, which required her to go between the buildings of the junior high campus. She took a friend with her. When she had retrieved her purse, the two girls began to walk back to PE. But her friend had also forgotten something, and left Kimberly outside to retrieve her item. When the friend got back, Kimberly was walking away with a man. The two had been seen by several other witnesses, but all chalked the presence of the "angry man" up to a simply cross father retrieving his daughter. But when the administrators of the school called home, they were met with confusion...and then fear. At first, the authorities thought this was simply a runaway case. But Kimberly was happy with her life, getting along well with her parents and a member of the Valentine's Court. Thinking back to the recent murders in Tallahassee, their investigation became more serious. It took seven weeks to find her body. It was discovered, half rotting and half mummified, in a pig pen near the Suwannee River State Park, 35 miles from Lake City. She showed signs of sexual assault and strangulation, but was otherwise free from signs of physical assault. This would be Ted Bundy's final kill in his life.

Although Bundy had been relatively successful in his kills while in Florida, he had been unlucky in his life otherwise. He was overdue on rent and low on cash, still living off of petty crime to survive. In addition, he had a growing suspicion that the police were onto him. On February 12, 1978, Bundy stole yet another car and fled Tallahassee. He drove west, along the line of the gulf en route to Alabama. Three days of driving later, at 1:00 am, he was finally caught by Officer David Lee in Pensacola. The officer had run the plates on Ted's stolen Beetle. When Officer Lee attempted to place Bundy under arrest, the frantic man kicked Lee's legs out from under him and bolted. Drawing his gun, Lee fired over Ted's head as a warning shot. He followed up with another, closer this time. He then chased down the still running Bundy, tackling him to the ground. Bundy tried to get as hold of the officer's gun, but was thwarted. Finally, Officer Lee was able to constrai Bundy with handcuffs and place him under arrest. While Bundy stewed in the backseat of his patrol car, Lee searched the stolen Beetle. Inside, there were student ID cards for three FSU students, 21 stolen credit cards, and a television set that Bundy had stolen fairly recently. He also found what turned out to be Ted's costume as "Richard Burton," a pair of sunglasses and a pair of plaid slacks. Bundy said only one thing as he was driven to the police headquarters.

"You should have killed me."

A Monster, Caged For Good

In June, 1979, Ted Bundy was yet again before a judge, this time in Miami. He was on trial for his actions at the Chi Omega house. The venue had been changed, as any trial in Tallahassee's jurisdiction would have led to a biased verdict. Bringing in one of the FBI's most wanted fugitives was a sensation at the time, and the trial was broadcast on television nationwide as well as covered by over 250 reporters from all over the world. Despite his predicament, Ted remained a control freak, demanding utmost control over his defense during the proceedings. Though he had 5 attorneys assigned to his case by the court, Bundy stubbornly remained the main lawyer for his own defense. At the start, one of Bundy's lawyers came up with a plea deal. If Bundy pleaded guilty to the murders of Levy, Leach, and Bowman then he would get a sentence of 75 years, no more and no less. The prosecution was amenable, and all it needed was Ted's agreement to go through. At first, he thought it to be a "tactical move," expecting the case against him to fall apart only a few years into his sentence and he would be exonerated.

But, as it had in the past, Ted's pride got in the way. No matter how smart of an idea the plea bargain may have been, it would have made Ted admit that he was guilty. He couldn't bring himself to do it.

The trial brought in multiple witnesses from the sorority house who had seen him in and around Chi Omega on the night of the murders. One of them, Nita Neary, recalled seeing him holding the piece of heavy oak he'd used as his blunt weapon. The prosecution had experts match the bite mark in Lisa Levy's buttock with casting s of Ted's teeth. The jury only needed 7 hours to proclaim Bundy guilty. He was convicted of the murders of Bowman and Levy, three counts of attempted first degree murder, and two counts of Burglary. He was given the death sentence. Six months later, Bundy faced yet another judge and jury for the murder of Kimberly Leach. At this trial, the prosecution could place him at Lake City Junior High the day of the abduction, with one witness seeing Bundy leave with Leach. There was also a match between fibers found on Leach and in Bundy's van that matched fibers from Bundy's jacket.

His guilt assured, the jury now needed to decide on if he should be executed. Ted knew he would be, but he had a more important thought on his mind. In his research for his case, he had come across an obscure law in Florida that stated a marriage declared in a court room in front of a judge was a legal marriage. The woman he would ask to marry him was easily accessible. Carol Anne Boone, his old flame and ex-co worker from Washington, had moved to Florida to be near Ted and hopefully rekindle their relationship. She had been a witness at both trials. Bundy popped the question while Boone was on the stand, a request added to a line of questioning asked by Ted as his own defense. She accepted, and Bundy proudly declared that they were now man and wife. They would stay married until his death.

In February of 1980, Bundy got his third death sentence, this for the murder of Leach. The method was to be execution, and it would be this sentence that killed him 9 years later. Ted, upon hearing the judgment, cried out that the jury had made some mistake. But there was nothing to be done. Ted Bundy would fry. Ted spent his remaining days at Railford Prison.

In 1982, while Bundy was in prison, Boone gave birth to a daughter. Bundy, she said, was the father. While conjugal visits were not allowed, inmates often saved up money and bribed guards into allowing unofficial ones.

Ted began his famous interviews while in prison, giving invaluable information to the world on his motives and the insight into the mind of a serial killer. But while he was appealing his case, a long an arduous process, Ted still planned an escape. Two guards had found a pair of hacksaws in his room, and that the bars over his window had been sawed in half and temporarily glued back together until Bundy needed to escape. He was moved cells.

Bundy was attacked in 1984 by his fellow inmates. No doubt his status as a child rapist and murder did nothing to endear him to the men on death row, nor did his smarmy attitude and relative fame. They attacked him in a group. While it was at least a violent assault, at least one source called in a gang rape.

Ted repeatedly engaged with modern crime while in prison. He took up a secret correspondence with John Hinkley Jr, for which he received a disciplinary infraction. Bundy thought himself to be an expert on serial killers, and offered himself up for interview to detectives investigating such incidents. He was taken up on his offer by the Washington Police, sending two officers to interview Bundy to gain insight on the pathology of the Green River Killer.

Considered by some to be Bundy's successor, Gary Ridgway operated in the same area as Bundy had. If Bundy helped at all, it wasn't enough. The Green River Killer remained at large for 17 years.

While he was meant to be executed on March 4th of 1986, he received a stay. When the date was rescheduled to July 2nd, Ted decided he no longer had a use for secrecy. He gave his most important confessions during what he thought were his final months on earth. He detailed his murders, his actions, and for the first time admitted to what he did to the corpses of his victims. Bundy was not satisfied in the murder of women. He needed to exert his control and possession over them, even in death. He visited the graves of his victims and lay with them in their shallow graves. Then he would perform sexual acts on the corpse. Sometimes he'd drive a long way and stay with the corpses all night. He repeated this until the body became too putrefied for him to continue. He admitted to shampooing some of their hair, or doing their makeup. He also admitted that he had decapitated at least 12 of his victims with a chainsaw, placing some of these heads in his car and taking them home. Four of them, the victims discovered on Taylor Mountain, were kept in his apartment until he either tired of them or they stank too bad to hide.

15 hours before his execution for the Chi Omega murder, the court remanded the case on multiple technicalities. The execution was delayed indefinitely. But he still had a death sentence for the murder of Leach. His appeal progressed through the courts,

receiving delay after delay on his execution. But the buck stopped in Washington, D.C. The Supreme Court declined to hear Bundy's case, meaning the finding of the lower court would hold firm. Ted had nowhere to go now, and his execution was set, for good, on January 24th, 1989.

After giving information on the kills they had confirmed, Bundy began to confess to murders that the police had no knowledge of. But this was yet another ruse by Bundy. He only told the interviewers enough to pique interest, not enough to prove anything. He intended to make himself too invaluable to these potential investigations to kills. But all it did was make the officers of the law want to see him executed sooner.

By the time of his death, the handsome Ted Bundy had many admirers. When these people heard that Ted would die, and that he had no other option, they begged the families in Oregon and Colorado to beg Florida Governor Martinez for clemency. The families, convinced of his part in the murders, declined.

Carol Boone has been Ted's biggest defender for some time, but when his confessions were released, she was heartbroken. She felt betrayed by Ted ,and she returned to Seattle with her daughter. Ted had one phone call before he went to the chair, and it was to Boone. She didn't take it.

Theodore Robery Bundy was executed by the state of Florida at 7:16 am EST, on January 24th of 1989. He was 42. The jail has been surrounded by revelers, and when news of his death reached them they erupted into cheers. The celebrants, including over 20 off duty police officers, danced and set off fireworks. They cheered twice as loud as the hearse carrying Bundy drove past. He was cremated in Gainesville and his ashes were spread across the Cascade Mountains. It had taken many tries, but Ted Bundy had finally answered for his crimes.

Who Was Ted Bundy?

Why was Bundy so successful> How
did it take so long for police to nail down a
murderer who had killed so many in such a
small amount of time? It was several factors.

As a law student, he knew the
methodologies of the police and knew how
to thwart them. He actively traveled between
kills, spreading his kills far and wide to
obscure their connection. It took twenty kills
before the various jurisdictions realized they
were all searching for the same killer. His
methods of murder were chosen to maximize
stealth. He killed using blunt weapons and
strangulation, silent methods that could be
done with a range of objects that all could
easily pass as common household items. He
never used a gun beyond threats, as the

noise and discharge would have been a great liability. He cased most of the places where he would commit murder extensively, planning his act out meticulously. He did the same with his storage sites, where he had to be sure they would not be easily discovered on purpose or otherwise. He was careful to never leave fingerprints, and the police never did find his prints at any crime scene. He used this fact repeatedly as evidence of his innocence.

Ted Bundy is often called a "chameleon," a moniker not without some merit. He was handsome, but generically so. He had the looks of an everyman, anonymous and easy to forget. He also had an uncanny skill at changing his face when needed, shaping his features to be different enough that he could be unidentifiable. In nearly every photo of Bundy, he looks different. He styled his hair in many different ways, and this alone could change his appearance.

But what was the mind of Bundy like? We know he had a fascination with women, whom he desired control over. But deep down he was severely antisocial. He had huge amounts of outward charisma but had no personality underneath. He could tell the difference between right and wrong, but it never had any effect. He never expressed remorse. He was narcissistic and manipulative.

Ted was not a serial killer for the sake of the kill. By his own confession, he had to get near black out drunk in order to go through with his murders. He coveted the women. He wanted to own them, to do as he pleased with them without the women speaking, contradicting him, or leaving him. When he returned to the bodies, he was always sober.

Ted never took responsibility for his crimes, even when it would have helped him. If he had shown remorse for the crimes at Chi Omega, for instance, he would have avoided the death sentence. Instead, Ted passed the buck. He blamed media, his grandfather's abuse, alcohol, society, true crime novels, and most famously, pornography. He blamed pornography for his violence in his final interview, which was grabbed onto by the Christian activist who'd interviewed hiim, James Dobson Ted's laying of his crimes at the feet of pornography led to a nationwide anti-porn movement.

Although actual psychologists and biographers of Bundy dismiss this idea, but the interview had been broadcast and the damage was done. For a long time afterward, porn and Ted Bundy would be linked.

Conclusion

There have been more prolific killers than Ted Bundy, and there have been more violent and sadistic killers than him as well. But who Ted was, the personality he exhibited and his general appearance meant he stood out in the American psyche. No longer was the idea of the serial killer a lurking monster, hidden in the dark and waiting to strike. The monsters could be handsome men, disguised as authority figures or pretending to be hurt. He changed our very idea of evil.

Bundy had an influence on media, his strange and sometimes ironic story being ripe fodder for Hollywood. He was played by Mark Harmon in a 1986 miniseries, released before his death, titled *The Deliberate*

Stranger. So successful was this series that author Anne Rule received voluminous fan mail from girls allegedly in love with the imprisoned Bundy. She had to remind them that Bundy was a murderer, and that they were in fact in love with the actor Mark Harmon. Three biopics have been made, most famously 2002's *Ted Bundy*, which starred Michael Reilly Burke in a chilling rendition of Bundy. Beyond adaptations of his story, his methods and personality were referenced and copied by many movies and TV shows. *Buffy the Vampire Slayer* had a whole episode called "Ted," where a handsome brown haired man hides a murderous personality beneath his a charming and kind facade. And in the Oscar winning horror film "The Silence of the Lambs," the killer Buffalo Bill used Bill's method of feigning injury to trap his victims. Bundy's actions as an attempted "expert" on killers like himself influence Hannibal Lecter's role as an FBI serial killer "expert." And no doubt the many handsome and friendly killers appearing across true crime media owe their performances to Ted Bundy.

Ted Bundy sits high in the rankings of killers. He had so many aspects that we as a society admire. He has handsome, charismatic, and ambitious. In a different life, he could have perhaps been a successful politician. But thanks to his pride, greed, cruelty, and lack of empathy he instead became one of history's greatest monsters. The name "Bundy" became synonymous with "killer." And it is not a stretch to wonder if he would have found some satisfaction in that fact.

Printed in Great Britain
by Amazon